I0072381

Medicare Supplement
vs.
Medicare Advantage

THE INSIDER'S GUIDE™ TO CHOOSING THE RIGHT PLAN FOR YOU

From the Author of *Prepare for Medicare*
The Insider's Guide® to Buying Medicare Insurance

Matt Feret

PART OF THE *THE INSIDER'S GUIDE*® SERIES

Medicare Supplement
vs.
Medicare Advantage

THE INSIDER'S GUIDE™ TO CHOOSING THE RIGHT PLAN FOR YOU

From the Author of *Prepare for Medicare*
The Insider's Guide® to Buying Medicare Insurance

Matt Feret

Designed by Dino Marino Design, dinomarinodesign.com

Printed in the United States of America

ISBN Print: 979-8-9879933-8-5
ISBN eBook: 979-8-9879933-9-2

LOOKING FOR A TRUSTED ADVISOR?

If you're already feeling overwhelmed or just want someone to walk you through this Medicare stuff, I've got someone I trust completely.

Her name is Niki. She's my wife – and a licensed, experienced, independent Medicare insurance agent and agency owner.

Now, recommending your spouse might sound a little biased, but hear me out. I'd recommend Niki even if I weren't married to her. I've seen the way she treats people. I've watched her build a boutique agency rooted in kindness, clarity, and no-pressure guidance. She runs the Brickhouse Agency, a small but mighty firm that helps people across the country navigate Medicare the right way – with no gimmicks, no shortcuts, and no pushy sales tactics.

She works with fully vetted, trusted insurance companies and donates 10% of her firm's annual net profit to charity. And she's helped thousands of people feel more confident, clearer, and more in control of their Medicare decisions.

WANT TO TALK TO SOMEONE LIKE THAT? HERE'S HOW:

- Visit www.BrickhouseAgency.com to schedule a free consultation – there's no obligation to enroll.

- Or call (844) 844-6565 to speak with someone to set an appointment.

- Prefer Zoom? Great. Prefer a phone call? That works too. (Camera off is always fine.)

If you already have an independent agent you love – stick with them! But if you don't, or you're not sure who to trust, Niki and her team are the first people I'd make an appointment with.

DISCLAIMER

This book is here to help you make smarter decisions about Medicare and retirement. It's based on my personal experience and opinions, formed over two decades working inside the healthcare and insurance industries. I've helped design plans, lead marketing and sales operations, train agents, and build tools used by millions of Medicare consumers.

That said, this book isn't legal, financial, tax, investment, or insurance advice. Everyone's situation is different, and you should always talk to licensed professionals who know your personal details before making decisions.

I'm not affiliated with or endorsed by the Social Security Administration, the Centers for Medicare & Medicaid Services (CMS), the Department of Health and Human Services, or any government agency. Any mention of government programs, companies, insurance carriers, or tools is strictly for education and illustration. Trademarks and brand names belong to their respective owners.

I do my best to make sure everything in this book is accurate and current. But Medicare and Social Security rules, premiums, and plan details change often – and sometimes quickly. That means something here may shift after publication.

I don't sell Medicare insurance. But I may reference trusted resources – like advisors, vendors, or consulting services – that I've personally vetted and believe in. Some of these may involve affiliate relationships or other partnerships. That never influences what I say. I only recommend what I'd feel good recommending to my own family.

The views expressed here are mine alone. They don't reflect any current or former employer, carrier, or agency I've worked with. This book was created independently and is not made by, on behalf of, or endorsed by any Medicare insurance carrier or government program.

Use your best judgment, ask good questions, and don't be afraid to get help. You're in charge of your financial decisions – and the more informed you are, the better those decisions will be.

TABLE OF CONTENTS

INTRODUCTION

Hi there – and thanks for spending your time with this book. Whether you're reading it, listening to it, or scrolling through it on a screen, I'm glad you're here.

I'm Matt Feret, and I help people make smarter decisions around Medicare, retirement, and everything that comes with growing older in today's world.

I don't sell Medicare insurance, and I don't work as an executive for health insurance companies anymore. But I spent more than 20 years working inside the healthcare and insurance industry – leading national Medicare marketing and sales operations, building educational tools used by millions of consumers, training thousands of licensed Medicare agents and call centers, and even helping develop Medicare Advantage plan designs.

If you've ever enrolled in a Medicare plan – or called a company to ask about one – there's a real chance you've interacted with something I helped build.

Now, I use that experience to teach what I wish more people knew before they enrolled. I write books, create online courses, and host *The Matt Feret Show*, where I cover Medicare, Social Security, caregiving, retirement, and what it really takes to live a healthy, wealthy, and wise life in midlife and beyond.

This book is part of my *Insider's Guide* series – and it's here to help you answer the #1 Medicare question nearly everyone asks: **"Which one is better – Medicare Supplement or Medicare Advantage?"**

Quick heads up: Medicare Supplement plans and Medigap plans are the same thing. The terms are used interchangeably, and I'll use both throughout the book so you're fluent in how real-world Medicare conversations actually work.

Now, back to the question. Which one is better?

Like most important decisions, the answer is: It depends. (Don't roll your eyes, I *knew* you saw that coming.)

That's where this guide comes in.

You'll learn:

- The real-world differences between Medigap and MAPD

- How those differences affect your care, costs, and choices

- What's changing behind the scenes in the industry (and why it matters)

- What to ask before you enroll – or switch

- And how to avoid the kinds of mistakes that are hard to undo later

If you're looking for more support, I've also created free checklists and video courses on:

- Choosing the right Medicare path

- Understanding Medicare Supplement vs. Medicare Advantage

- Working with Medicare while still employed

- And other real-life scenarios most people eventually face

You'll find all of that – and more – at:

- ✅ PrepareforMedicare.com

- ✅ PrepareforSocialSecurity.com

- ✅ TheMattFeretShow.com

You can also hop on my free newsletter. I send out Medicare tips, Social Security explainers, retirement tools, and random-but-useful thoughts about living well in the second half of life.

Just once a month. No spam. No nonsense.

(I unsubscribe from that stuff, too.)

It's free, it's helpful, and I think you'll like it.

You're smart to be here. Most people don't take the time to learn how this all really works – and they pay for it, one way or another.

Let's make sure that's not you.

Here's to your wealth, wisdom, and wellness!

– Matt

THE PREPARE FOR MEDICARE INSIDER METHOD™

A 5-STEP SYSTEM FOR CONFIDENT MEDICARE DECISIONS

Choosing between Medicare Supplement (Medigap) and Medicare Advantage isn't just about comparing plans, it's about understanding where that decision fits in the broader Medicare journey.

That's where the *The Prepare for Medicare Insider Method™* comes in.

This five-step system was built from decades inside the Medicare and insurance world. It's designed to help you avoid mistakes, save money, and choose a Medicare path that actually fits your life.

This book focuses on Step 3 – *Choose the Right Coverage Path* – the point where most people get confused or misled.

Here's how the full Method breaks down:

STEP 1: LEARN THE LANDSCAPE

Understand the difference between Original Medicare, Medigap, Medicare Advantage, and Part D.

STEP 2: KNOW YOUR TIMING

Whether you're turning 65, still working, or already enrolled, the right timing matters.

STEP 3: CHOOSE THE RIGHT COVERAGE PATH

This step – your focus in this book – helps you weigh the real-world pros, cons, and trade-offs of Medicare Supplement vs. Medicare Advantage.

STEP 4: CHOOSE THE RIGHT INSURANCE COMPANY

Not all plans or carriers are created equal. Learn how to separate the trusted from the risky.

STEP 5: ANNUAL MEDICARE HOUSEKEEPING

Once you're enrolled, make sure your coverage still fits, especially during the Annual Election Period.

This book is your **Step 3 guide,** and it's part of the full system I teach in my courses, books, and content.

When you follow the Method, you're not missing anything. You're making Medicare work for you – on your terms, with insider clarity.

(And yes, there's a Bonus Chapter at the end that covers Step 4, too.)

CHAPTER 1

WHY THIS CHOICE MATTERS

Medicare Supplement and Medicare Advantage plans are two completely different ways to get additional Medicare coverage – but 99% of people turning 65 only ask one question:

"Which one should I get?"

And that's the right question. But the wrong time to ask it is after you've already enrolled.

This chapter sets the stage. It's going to tell you what's at stake, what you're allowed to do (and when), and how you can *accidentally lock yourself out* of one of these choices forever.

So, if you take nothing else from this book, remember this: when it comes to Medicare Supplements *in particular*, the timing of your decision really matters.

MEDICARE SUPPLEMENT = MEDIGAP (LET'S GET THAT STRAIGHT)

You'll hear the terms "Medicare Supplement" and "Medigap" used interchangeably – and that's because they're the same thing. These are private insurance policies that fill in the gaps of Original Medicare Part A and B.

Some agents and companies prefer "Medigap." Some prefer "Medicare Supplement." But they mean the same thing. This book uses both to keep things conversational – but just know they're not different products.

MAPD plans – Medicare Advantage plans that include drug coverage – are completely different from Medicare Supplement plans.

They don't fill in the gaps of Original Medicare like Medigap does. Instead, when you enroll in an MAPD plan, your Medicare benefits are administered and managed by a private insurance company rather than the federal government.

You're still technically enrolled in Original Medicare Part A and Part B, but the insurance company now runs the show. That means you follow their rules, use their network, and deal with their billing systems.

You'll choose one path or the other:

- ✅ Original Medicare + Medigap + Part D (standalone)
- ✅ MAPD (Medicare Advantage Plan with drug coverage built in)

That's the core of this book. And your choice here matters more than most people realize.

YOU MIGHT ONLY GET ONE SHOT AT MEDIGAP

If you're just turning 65 or enrolling in Medicare Part B for the first time, you're in your Medigap Open Enrollment Period – a six-month window that guarantees you can buy any Medicare Supplement policy available in your state without answering health questions.

Once this window closes, most people must go through underwriting to get a Medigap plan – meaning they'll be asked about their medical history and can be denied coverage, charged more, or offered fewer plan choices.

BUT THERE *ARE* EXCEPTIONS

While the Medigap Open Enrollment Period is the best time to get any plan with no health questions, there are other times you might qualify for a Medigap plan **without medical underwriting**:

- ✓ If you move out of your Medicare Advantage plan's service area

- ✓ If your MAPD plan exits the market

- ✓ If you try an MAPD plan and switch back within 12 months (trial right)

- ✓ If you drop a Medigap plan to try MAPD and switch back within 12 months (trial right)

- ✓ If your employer, union, or COBRA coverage ends

- ✓ Or if your plan misleads you or breaks Medicare rules

Some states – like New York, Connecticut, and Maine – also offer year-round or more flexible enrollment options. But those are the exception, not the rule.

This is why I say you may only get one shot at enrolling in a Medigap plan. If you don't take it, you may not get another chance.

STATE-SPECIFIC EXCEPTIONS (BUT DON'T COUNT ON THEM)

Some states have extra consumer protections:

Some states offer additional consumer protections – but usually only if you already have a Medigap plan.

- ✔ **California and Oregon** have a "birthday rule" that lets you switch to a different Medigap plan with equal or lesser benefits – without underwriting – each year around your birthday.

- ✔ **Missouri** has an "anniversary rule" that allows you to change Medigap carriers (but not plan types) around your plan anniversary.

- ✔ A few other states offer limited switching opportunities or ongoing guaranteed issue, but again – these mostly apply **only if you're already in a Medigap plan**.

But again – these are the exceptions – not the rules. Most people won't be eligible for guaranteed Medigap enrollment after that six-month window unless they qualify for specific situations (like losing employer coverage or moving).

REAL STORY: LOCKED OUT AFTER CANCER

I once spoke with a woman who turned 65 and chose a $0 Medicare Advantage plan. It worked well for her for a couple of years – until she was diagnosed with cancer.

She quickly learned that many of her preferred doctors didn't take her plan. The preauthorization process delayed treatments. And when she called about switching to a Medigap plan, she was told she'd have to go through underwriting.

She was declined by multiple companies.

The plan that would've let her go to any Medicare doctor with no questions asked was now off the table. She didn't understand that her one shot had already passed.

Matt Tip: Good health is temporary. Your plan shouldn't be.

Why You're Smart to Be Here Now

This decision – Medigap vs. MAPD – is not just about premiums and networks. It's about how you want to experience healthcare for the rest of your life.

Medigap gives you flexibility, nationwide access, and stable benefits. MAPD gives you lower premiums, built-in extras, and structured rules.

Neither is "bad." But one will fit you better than the other.

And if you're reading this before you make your decision? You're ahead of the game.

Most people don't ask until they've already enrolled – and by then, one of the options may no longer be available.

A Note About the Bigger Picture

This book focuses exclusively on this one, giant, confusing question – Medicare Supplement or Medicare Advantage?

If you want a full walk-through of how Medicare works – Parts A, B, C, D, penalties, timelines, IRMAA, and all the rest – check out my full-length book *Prepare for Medicare – The Insider's Guide® to Buying Medicare Insurance* or visit <u>PrepareforMedicare.com</u>.

I also created a video course that walks through this topic in even more detail – with examples, visuals, and voiceovers from me!

But here? We're zooming in on the most important – and often irreversible – Medicare decision most people face.

CHAPTER 2

WHAT ORIGINAL MEDICARE COVERS – AND WHAT IT DOESN'T

Before we can compare Medicare Supplement and Medicare Advantage plans, we need to step back and look at what they're trying to fill – or fix. That means understanding what Original Medicare actually covers… and what it doesn't.

You don't have to memorize every deductible and copay. But you *do* need to know where the gaps are. Because when you don't know the gaps, you can't protect yourself from them – and those gaps can get expensive.

WHAT ORIGINAL MEDICARE *DOES* COVER

Original Medicare is made up of two parts:

- ✅ Part A (Hospital Insurance): Covers inpatient hospital stays, limited time in skilled nursing facilities, some home health care, and hospice.

- ✅ Part B (Medical Insurance): Covers outpatient care, doctor visits, physical therapy, durable medical equipment, lab work, and preventive services.

Part A is generally premium-free for most people. Part B has a monthly premium that's income-based and typically comes out of your Social Security check.

WHAT ORIGINAL MEDICARE *DOESN'T* COVER

This list is longer – and maybe more important – than what's covered.

- ✅ No out-of-pocket maximum. There's no MOOP (Maximum Out-of-Pocket) limit. Your bills can keep stacking up.

- ✅ No prescription drug coverage. That's Part D, and it's a separate policy you must add, by way of a standalone Part D plan, or embedded into a Medicare Advantage (MA**PD**) plan.

- ✅ No routine dental, vision, or hearing care. These are on you unless you add other coverage.

- ✅ No long-term custodial care. If you need help bathing, eating, or dressing long-term, Medicare won't pay for it. Same for long-term care.

- ✅ No international coverage (with a few rare exceptions).

This is why people either:

1. Add a Medigap plan and standalone Part D, or

2. Join a Medicare Advantage plan that wraps in drug coverage and extra benefits.

Matt Tip: Original Medicare is a good foundation – but it's not a complete insurance policy.

THE BIG GAPS – AND THE BIG RISKS

Let's put some numbers behind it.

- ✅ Part A hospital deductible: Several hundred dollars per benefit period – and you could pay this more than once per year.

- ✅ Part A coinsurance after 60 days in hospital: Daily charges increase the longer you stay, and once you hit your lifetime reserve days, you could be responsible for the full cost.

- ✅ Skilled nursing facility coinsurance: After a short fully covered period, you'll start paying a daily rate that adds up quickly.

  Important: Medicare only covers skilled nursing facility care **if you've had a qualifying three-day inpatient hospital stay first**. Observation stays don't count – even if you spent the night in the hospital. That's a common and expensive surprise if you're not aware of the rule.

- ✅ Part B coinsurance: You pay 20% of all covered services – and there's no cap.

That means if you have major surgery or spend time in the hospital or a skilled nursing facility, you could easily be on the hook for thousands – or tens of thousands – of dollars.

Even common situations can get expensive:

- ✅ A simple surgery + rehab can trigger the hospital deductible, 20% outpatient costs, and skilled nursing coinsurance.

- ✅ Physical therapy or infusion treatments? You're paying 20% each time.

- ✅ Durable medical equipment like a walker or CPAP? 20%.

- ✅ Expensive injectable or IV medications (like Prolia, chemotherapy, or certain osteoporosis drugs)? They're billed under Part B – not Part D – and you'll owe 20% unless you have a Medigap plan.

REAL STORY: THE EXPENSIVE FALL

Years ago, I met a woman during a Medicare education seminar who had slipped and fallen. She was hospitalized and needed several weeks in a skilled nursing facility. She had Original Medicare only – no Medigap or MAPD.

Medicare Part A paid for the first 20 days at 100%, but after that, she was responsible for over $200 per day. She stayed 47 days total. That's over $5,000 out of pocket just for the facility – before factoring in the hospital deductible, prescriptions, and outpatient rehab.

She thought Medicare would cover it all. Oh, it covered it, but it didn't pay for it all.

ANOTHER REAL STORY: RUNNING OUT OF LIFETIME RESERVE DAYS

I once spoke with a woman whose close friend was hospitalized for over a year. The friend had multiple amputations; it was horrible. She called me in a panic, as they used up all 60 of their lifetime reserve days under Medicare Part A – and once those were gone, Medicare stopped paying for the hospital stay entirely.

The family had no Medigap policy to fall back on and ended up responsible for tens of thousands of dollars in bills. When they called me, they were in the middle of looking for charitable organizations and state-based assistance organizations for options. Just an awful situation.

That's rare – but it's real.

COMMON MISCONCEPTIONS ABOUT WHAT MEDICARE COVERS

A surprising number of people assume that Medicare includes benefits like:

- Annual eye exams or eyeglasses
- Hearing aids
- Routine dental cleanings or dentures
- Long-term care in a nursing home

It doesn't.

Some MAPD plans offer limited versions of these benefits – but Original Medicare Parts A and B do not. If you want this coverage, you'll have to get it elsewhere.

Matt Tip: Don't assume Medicare covers something just because you've always had it through an employer plan.

A WORD ON IRMAA AND THE PART B AND PART D PREMIUMS

While not a coverage gap, many people are surprised to find out their Part B and Part D premiums can increase based on income. This is called IRMAA – Income-Related Monthly Adjustment Amount.

If you're a higher-income individual or couple, your Medicare premiums may be higher than the standard amount due to IRMAA – the Income-Related Monthly Adjustment Amount. IRMAA applies to both Part B and Part D premiums.

Most people first run into IRMAA the year after they stop working, when their tax return still reflects full-time income. That's usually when the notice shows up in the mail – right about the time you're thinking your retirement cashflow budget is all set – and suddenly, there's a line item you didn't plan for.

You look at it and think, *"Wait… what is this?"*

If you've had a recent income drop due to retirement, divorce, the death of a spouse, or a work reduction, you may be able to appeal IRMAA using Form SSA-44. It's Social Security's way of letting you say, "Hey, that old tax return doesn't reflect my income anymore."

Most Medicare agents can point you to the form, but they can't give tax advice or talk to the Social Security Administration on your behalf. If you want help navigating the appeal process, I've partnered with a team that does this every day. You can find them at PrepareforMedicare.com/irmaa. The initial consultation is free, and if you move forward, there's a fee for the service.

Matt Tip: You're not stuck with IRMAA forever. But you have to know it exists – and know how to challenge it.

REAL LIFE EXAMPLES: WHAT HAPPENS AFTER THE BROCHURES

JOE & LINDA: TWO ONE-SHOT PATHS

Joe and Linda were high-school teachers who retired the same year. Both had similar health histories and financial situations.

- ✅ **Joe chose Medicare Supplement Plan G**, paying about $160/month for unmatched provider flexibility – no referrals, no network questions.

- ✅ **Linda selected a $0-premium Medicare Advantage PPO**, enjoying extras like dental and OTC cards with an annual dollar allowance.

Two years later, Linda needed knee surgery. Her surgeon and imaging center were **in-network**, but the pain specialist she used for follow-up was out-of-network. Her PPO allowed it – but only at **50% coinsurance after a deductible**. That meant:

1. She hit a separate $500 out-of-pocket deductible for out-of-network care, then

2. Paid 50% of all ongoing specialist bills, meaning a $300 specialist visit cost her $150.

Despite her initial formula, Linda ended up paying nearly **$1,200 extra in out-of-pocket** costs that year – on top of her Part B premium and medications.

Meanwhile, Joe had his surgery and follow-ups without surprise bills – his only costs were the standard Part B deductible and Plan G-covered coinsurance.

Matt Tip: Zero premium is tempting. But how many times do you want to ask yourself, 'Is this worth the network trade-off?'

THREE MINI-STORIES THAT CHANGED THE PLAN

1. Frank the Snowbird

Frank winters in Florida and summers in Minnesota. His PPO MAPD let him see providers in both states – but Florida specialists weren't in-network. After a routine cardiology appointment, he met the $500 out-of-network deductible, then paid **50% coinsurance** on every visit. A $600 bill became $300 out-of-pocket – after already paying $800 elsewhere. Flexibility can come with steep costs.

Matt Tip: If you split time between places, ask how much out-of-network care actually costs before relying on flexibility.

2. Barbara and the Diabetes Denial

Barbara chose a $0-premium MAPD plan and liked it – until she was diagnosed with diabetes. She wanted to switch to Medigap but was **denied for health reasons** and missed her trial window. She was locked into a plan that no longer matched her needs.

Matt Tip: Health changes don't qualify you for a do-over. Locking into a low-cost plan early can backfire later.

3. Tom's Surprise at the Cancer Center

Tom assumed his MAPD plan covered nationally recognized hospitals. It didn't. His chosen cancer center was out-of-network, requiring phone calls, special permission and when approved, and steep coinsurance. Routine appointments that he thought were covered ended up costing hundreds.

Matt Tip: Just because a plan name sounds big doesn't mean your doctor is in it – or that nationally-recognized hospital systems will be in-network.

WHY THIS CHAPTER MATTERS

Everything in the rest of this book builds on this foundation:

- ✅ Medigap plans cover most of these gaps but come with higher premiums.

- ✅ MAPD plans offer lower premiums and extras – but introduce rules, networks, and preapprovals.

This is why neither path is "better" – they're just different ways to fill the same holes in Original Medicare.

Now let's dig into how Medigap plans work – and why they remain a popular option even as Medicare Advantage popularity grows.

CHAPTER 3

MEDICARE SUPPLEMENT PLANS (MEDIGAP)

Medicare Supplement plans – also called Medigap plans – work alongside Original Medicare to cover many of the costs Medicare doesn't. These include deductibles, coinsurance, and copayments. The goal is financial predictability and freedom to choose your doctors.

This chapter will walk you through:

- ☑ What Medigap plans cover (and don't)
- ☑ Which Medigap plans are most popular (and why)
- ☑ How much they cost – and how those costs grow
- ☑ Why Medigap pricing works the way it does

✅ Insider insight into why some agents don't promote certain options

By the end, you'll understand why Medigap plans are the preferred choice for many – and why others pass on them.

Want to know how to evaluate the insurance company behind the plan – not just the letter on the card? Be sure to check out the Bonus Chapter at the end: "How to Read an Insurance Company (Like an Insider)."

HOW MEDIGAP PLANS WORK

Medigap plans only work if you stay on Original Medicare Parts A and B. They don't replace your Medicare benefits – they supplement them.

If Medicare covers something, your Medigap plan typically picks up most (or all) of what's left over. If Medicare doesn't cover it, your Medigap plan doesn't either.

There's no network. You can go to any doctor or hospital in the country that accepts Medicare. There's no gatekeeping, no referral requirements, and no preauthorizations.

WHAT MEDIGAP PLANS COVER

All Medigap plans are standardized by the government. That means Plan G from one insurance company has the same benefits as Plan G from another.

The most popular Medigap plans:

- ✅ Plan G: Covers almost everything except the Medicare Part B deductible

- ✅ Plan N: Similar to Plan G but with small copays and no excess charge coverage

- ✅ High-Deductible Plan G: Same benefits as Plan G after a high deductible is met (a favorite of mine – we'll get to why)

Note: A few states – like **Wisconsin, Massachusetts, and Minnesota** – have their own unique versions of Medigap plans that don't follow the standard plan letter system. If you live in one of those states, the general concepts still apply, but the plan names and structures will look a little different.

Why People Like Medigap

- ✅ Freedom to choose providers: No networks – go where you want

- ✅ Predictable costs: Few or no surprise bills

- ✅ No referrals or preapprovals: Direct access to specialists

✅ Nationwide portability: Great for snowbirds and travelers

Medigap plans are great for people who value access, flexibility, and financial predictability – even if they cost more than MAPD plans.

THE COST OF MEDIGAP

This is the part many people skip: Medigap plans come with monthly premiums, and those premiums increase over time.

Let's say you start Plan G at age 65 for $150/month. That could grow to:

✅ $180/month by age 70

✅ $230/month by age 75

✅ $300+/month by your 80s or 90s

That's before you add in the Part D drug plan and IRMAA fees, if applicable.

Every company files rate increases with your state, and those increases are often percentage-based, meaning the more your premium grows, the bigger the dollar increase year to year.

Matt Tip: A 15% increase on $300 premium hurts more than 15% on a $60 premium. It's not just the percentage – it's the dollar impact.

REAL STORY: TWO FRIENDS, SAME PLAN G – VERY DIFFERENT PRICES

I once worked with two clients who both had Plan G. Same benefits. Same ZIP Code. One paid $180/month, the other paid $250/month.

The difference? One bought her policy directly from a big, well-known company's website – and paid higher premiums. The other worked with an independent agent who shopped around for a better deal. Both plans worked the same. But over time, the cost difference was huge.

That's why working with a good independent agent matters. They can compare companies – not just recommend one carrier they happen to work with.

PLAN N – A SOLID MIDDLE GROUND

Plan N is a great choice for people who don't mind paying small copays ($20 for a doctor visit, $50 for ER) and want lower premiums than Plan G. The tradeoff? It doesn't cover Medicare Part B excess charges – but many doctors don't bill those anyway.

Plan N is often overlooked, but it's growing in popularity – especially among people entering Medicare who want value and are comfortable with a little more cost-sharing.

A WORD ABOUT HIGH-DEDUCTIBLE PLAN G

My opinion? This plan doesn't get enough love.

You pay a much lower premium – sometimes under $50/month – and only pay out of pocket until you hit the annual deductible (right around $3,000 these days). After that, it acts like full Plan G.

If you're healthy and want a Medigap plan but can't stomach $200+/month premiums, this can be a great solution.

But here's the problem: many agents don't mention High-Deductible Plan G. Why? Because they're paid on a percentage of premium – and $50/month earns a lot less than $150/month.

That's not a knock on agents. It's just the math. If yours doesn't bring it up, ask them.

WHY COMPANY SIZE MATTERS

Medigap plans are regulated at the state level, but companies vary wildly in experience, size, and service.

If a company doesn't have at least 100,000 Medigap policyholders, it may lack:

- Strong financials to withstand big claims

- Experienced leadership and Medicare-specific teams

- ✅ Investment in customer service or claims support

Smaller companies often outsource everything – customer service, underwriting, even claims handling – which can lead to a more frustrating experience when something goes wrong.

They may not care much about fixing issues. With fewer policyholders, they may not even have full-time Medicare-dedicated teams.

If you want to go deeper into how to evaluate a Medigap company from the inside – leadership, claims practices, red flags – I cover that in more detail in the Bonus Chapter.

Matt Tip: Small companies may have low premiums to get in the game – but they often don't have the people, budget, or systems to play long-term.

WHAT MEDIGAP DOESN'T COVER

It's worth repeating: Medigap only pays after Medicare pays. So, it won't help with:

- ✅ Prescription drugs (you'll need a standalone Part D plan)
- ✅ Dental, vision, or hearing insurance

✅ Long-term care coverage

That's why you'll often hear people refer to the full setup as "Original Medicare + Medigap + Part D."

You'll need all three pieces to feel protected – and that adds up in both premiums and complexity.

WHY AGENTS DON'T ALWAYS RECOMMEND MEDIGAP

Let's be honest – Medigap can be more complex to explain, harder to underwrite, and lower-paying for agents (especially High-Deductible Plan G).

Some agents don't get trained on Medigap. Some can only sell one company's plan. Some would rather steer everyone to MAPD because it's faster, easier, and usually pays a higher commission.

This doesn't mean those agents are bad people. But it does mean you need to know what to ask – and what's available.

In the next chapter, we'll cover how Medicare Advantage works – and why so many people are choosing it today.

CHAPTER 4

MEDICARE ADVANTAGE PLANS (MAPD)

Medicare Advantage plans – also known as MAPD plans when they include drug coverage – are an all-in-one alternative to Original Medicare. You still enroll in Medicare Part A and B, but the insurance company you choose becomes your primary coverage provider.

Think of it this way: when you enroll in an MAPD plan, you're handing the keys to your Medicare over to a private company. They're now in charge of managing your care – and your costs.

In this chapter, we'll walk through:

- ✅ How MAPD plans work
- ✅ Why they're so popular (and why they're growing)

✅ The benefits they offer – and what strings are attached

✅ How networks, preapprovals, and plan changes really work

✅ What to look for (and look out for)

By the end, you'll see why some people love MAPD plans – and why others run from them.

WHAT MAPD PLANS ARE (AND ARE NOT)

MAPD plans are not Medigap plans. They don't supplement Original Medicare – they run it. When you enroll in an MAPD plan, your Medicare coverage is handled by a private insurance company, not the federal government.

With MAPD, you still pay your Part B premium (and possibly Part A if applicable), but your care is managed by the insurance company. That means:

✅ You'll follow their rules

✅ You'll use their network

✅ You'll be subject to their coverage policies

MAPD plans are county-based – not national or even state-wide. Plans and insurance agents use ZIP Codes to quote eligibility, but they're approved at the county level. That's why plan availability can vary dramatically – even across nearby towns.

WHAT MAPD PLANS USUALLY INCLUDE

- ✔ Medical coverage (replacing Original Medicare)

- ✔ Built-in Part D prescription drug coverage

- ✔ Extras like dental, vision, hearing, gym memberships, transportation, or OTC cards

- ✔ Set copays for doctor visits, ER, hospital stays, and more

WHAT MAKES MAPD PLANS APPEALING

- ✔ Low (or $0) monthly premiums

- ✔ All-in-one convenience

- ✔ Extras that Original Medicare doesn't offer

- ✔ Annual Maximum Out-of-Pocket (MOOP) limits, which cap your financial exposure

That MOOP number is important. It's the maximum you'll pay in a calendar year for covered medical services. Once you hit it, the plan pays 100%.

But keep in mind: MOOP doesn't include drug costs, dental/vision/hearing, or out-of-network expenses unless your plan says so.

REAL STORY: PREAUTHORIZATION DELAY FOR SURGERY

A man I met had a Medicare Advantage plan that required preauthorization for outpatient surgery. His doctor submitted the request… and waited.

The insurance company dragged its feet. Calls weren't returned. The approval came – but not until two weeks after his originally scheduled date.

Nothing catastrophic happened – but the delay caused anxiety, rescheduling headaches, and frustration.

That's the tradeoff. MAPD plans offer structure and lower premiums, but you're agreeing to play by the insurance company's rules.

PART B GIVEBACK PLANS

You've probably seen these advertised: "Get $100 back in your Social Security check!"

These are Part B giveback plans – MAPD plans that reduce the amount of your Part B premium. Instead of $0 premium, you get less than zero because the plan gives you money back.

But there's always a tradeoff.

- ✅ The giveback might come with fewer benefits elsewhere

- ✅ The plan's drug coverage might not be as strong

- ✅ The network may be narrower

Nothing is truly free. Giveback plans can be great – but only if the rest of the plan works for your health and medications.

Matt Tip: If you're being "paid" to join a Medicare plan, ask yourself what you're agreeing to in return.

WHAT YOU NEED TO KNOW ABOUT MAPD NETWORKS

Unlike Medigap, which has no networks, MAPD plans have very specific provider networks. These are often:

- ✅ HMO (Health Maintenance Organization): Must stay in network except for emergencies. Referrals are usually required.

✅ PPO (Preferred Provider Organization): Can go out-of-network, but it'll cost you more.

Even in PPO plans, your costs are lower in-network. But here's the kicker: many people don't know whether their doctors or hospitals are in the plan's network – and networks can change every year.

Worse, provider directories are often outdated or just plain wrong. Remember how annoying it was on your employer health plan to find an in-network doctor – only to call and find out the number was disconnected, the doctor had moved, or they weren't actually in-network after all?

That same mess exists in Medicare Advantage plans, too. The printed directories are often outdated the moment they're published, and even the online tools aren't always accurate.

REAL STORY: "IN-NETWORK" HOSPITAL – UNTIL IT WASN'T

A couple I once talked to chose an MAPD plan that listed their local hospital as in-network. Months later, they got a letter saying the contract was ending. Suddenly, their hospital was no longer covered.

The plan and hospital couldn't come to an agreement, and the couple had to find a new facility – or switch plans.

That's becoming more common. As more people enroll in MAPD plans, more hospitals and provider groups are pushing back – sending termination notices, demanding higher reimbursement from the insurance companies, or pulling out of accepting any Medicare Advantage plans entirely.

You may even see this play out in the local newspaper with op-eds or press releases. And if you're caught in the middle? Tough luck.

Matt Tip: Networks aren't forever. What's in today might be out tomorrow – especially in MAPD.

LEADERSHIP, OUTSOURCING, AND WHAT YOU DON'T SEE IN THE BROCHURES

The quality of your Medicare Advantage plan often comes down to something you'll never see in the TV ads: who's running the company – and how well they understand Medicare Advantage.

I've worked inside companies where the leadership team didn't fully grasp how Medicare Advantage actually works. The claims systems were neglected. The provider relationships were shaky. The teams managing quality scores and member experience? Outsourced. Underfunded. Overwhelmed.

That's not unusual – especially in smaller companies. They may outsource everything from claims to provider networks to Star Rating management. And if they don't have the scale or expertise to manage those vendors well? You're the one who feels it when things fall apart.

Company size matters. So do leadership experience and execution. And while Medicare Star Ratings (1 to 5 Stars) give you a general idea of plan quality, they don't tell the full story. Some small companies launch with solid ratings but quickly slide once the complexity kicks in.

Want to know what to look for behind the scenes – how to tell the difference between a solid plan and a shaky one? I go deeper on that in the Bonus Chapter: *How to Read an Insurance Company (Like an Insider).*

Matt Tip: If a company can't keep a 4-star rating, they probably shouldn't keep your trust either.

WHAT HAPPENS IF YOUR HEALTH CHANGES?

Here's a hard truth: MAPD plans work best for people who don't use them much.

If you're healthy, great. But if your health changes – if you need surgeries, specialists, infusions, or rehab – you'll be navigating:

- ✅ Prior authorizations
- ✅ Network restrictions
- ✅ Out-of-pocket costs up to your MOOP

And if your plan's network shrinks or your doctor leaves? You're stuck until the next Annual Election Period.

REAL STORY: THE CANCER CURVEBALL

A woman in her late 60s had an MAPD plan that worked fine for years. Then she was diagnosed with cancer. Her preferred oncologist wasn't in-network. The cancer center was out-of-network. She needed preapprovals for every scan, drug, and follow-up visit.

It was exhausting – and expensive.

She wanted to switch to Medigap – but was denied coverage due to her new diagnosis.

This is one of the biggest risks with MAPD. It may work great now – but if your health shifts, your options may narrow.

IN SUMMARY

MAPD PLANS ARE GROWING FAST FOR A REASON:

- They're affordable

- They're convenient

- They offer benefits Original Medicare doesn't

But they're not for everyone.

In a sense, you're trading freedom for structure, and low premiums for higher out-of-pocket risk.

In the next chapter, we'll compare these paths side by side over time – so you can see the financial differences in action.

CHAPTER 5

WHAT THIS COULD COST YOU OVER TIME

Let's go deeper on the dollars. Because that's why you're here, right? When people ask, "Which plan is better?" they're really asking, "What's going to cost me more in the long run?"

Let's do a thought exercise:

- ✔ Suppose you start with a Medicare Supplement Plan G at $150/month, plus a stand-alone Part D plan at $20/month. That's $170/month or $2,040/year. And that premium is going to rise – assume a modest 3% to 5% increase per year (though in reality, some years could be 10%+).

✓ On the other side, say you enroll in a MAPD plan with a $0 or $20 monthly premium. That's $0 – $240/year. Big difference upfront.

But now ask: how many years would you need to hit the Maximum Out-of-Pocket (MOOP) under the MAPD plan – let's say $7,000 – for it to match what you'd spend in Medigap premiums?

Let's assume no major issues for five years. You're "winning" on the MAPD side. But if you hit the MOOP just once every four or five years, the math starts to swing – especially when you factor in:

✓ Higher copays along the way

✓ Fewer network choices

✓ Prior authorizations that delay or block care

✓ The real risk of plan exit or network disruption

Meanwhile, that Medigap plan is quietly humming along. You pay more each month, but there are no network worries, minimal out-of-pocket medical bills, and nearly predictable annual costs.

HERE'S THE "INSIDER" WAY TO THINK ABOUT IT:

Medigap = Pay more now, worry less later

MAPD = Pay less now, hope it works out later

It's not just about health or even wealth. Even wealthy people go the MAPD route because:

- ✅ They're healthy now

- ✅ They know how to play the "switch game" during AEPs

- ✅ They want to experiment for a few years while Medigap is still an option

But if you wait too long and get denied later (due to health), that "experiment" becomes permanent.

Let's talk about inflation. That $150/month Medigap premium you start with at age 65? It doesn't stay that low. Premiums usually increase with age, and on top of that, they often go up 3–5% each year due to medical inflation.

By age 80, that $150 can easily become $350/ month – that's over $4,000 a year just for Medigap. Add a $35/month Part D plan, and now you're paying more than $4,400/year just to stay insured.

Have a spouse on the same setup? Double it. That's nearly $9,000 a year.

Yikes.

And that's just premiums. That doesn't include deductibles, copays, or anything else you might need along the way.

Meanwhile, many MAPD premiums might remain $0–$40/month. But those MOOPs keep rising, too. Today's $7,000 could be $9,500 or more by then. And you may not be healthy enough to switch anymore.

Matt Tip: The best plan isn't always the cheapest one. It's the one that fits your health, your finances, and your peace of mind.

When comparing costs, look beyond year one. Think about your 70s and 80s – not just your first few years on Medicare. Think about:

- ✓ How you'd handle a $5,000 or $7,000 surprise

- ✓ What peace of mind is worth

- ✓ And what access and simplicity are worth as your care needs grow

If the Medigap premium fits in your budget – now and down the road – it's hard to beat the predictability. But if it stretches you too thin? Don't force it. An MAPD plan might make more sense – as long as you review it annually and know the trade-offs.

Bottom line: there's no free lunch in Medicare. But there is clarity – if you know how to do the math over time.

Insider Insight: What to Do When Medigap Gets Pricey

At age 65, enrolling in a Medicare Supplement (Medigap) plan can feel like a smart, safe decision – and for many people, it is. The coverage is predictable, the out-of-pocket costs are low, and you don't have to deal with provider networks or prior authorization hassles.

But here's something a lot of people don't think about at enrollment – and don't usually discover until years later: those premiums go up. Sometimes a little. Sometimes a lot.

Most Medigap plans use attained-age pricing, which means your premium increases as you get older. And even if you have a different pricing model-like issue-age or community-rated-insurers can still raise premiums due to medical inflation, changes in claims trends, or state-level pricing adjustments.

A couple might both enroll in Plan G at age 65 and feel comfortable with the monthly premium. But fast-forward six or seven years, and now they're both in their early 70s. Their combined Medigap premiums might be hundreds of dollars more each month than when they started – and that can hit hard, especially on a fixed income.

It's not unusual for people to start wondering: *"Is it time to look at something with a lower monthly cost – like a Medicare Advantage Plan?"*

Maybe. But be careful.

A lower-cost Medicare Advantage Plan (MAPD) might help reduce monthly premiums – but as you know by now, it's a very different kind of plan. And more importantly, once you leave Medigap, it may be very hard to get back in.

Unless you qualify for a special guaranteed issue right – or you're still within your 12-month "trial right" (the one-time option to go back to Medigap after trying MAPD) – you'll need to go through medical underwriting to return. And underwriting? It usually gets harder the older you get.

That's why it's smart to think long-term when choosing a Medigap plan at 65 – and to check in every few years to see how your plan is holding up.

If you're at that point now – where the Medigap premiums are starting to bite – it may be time to compare your current plan to Medicare Advantage options and weigh the trade-offs.

If you already work with a licensed agent you trust, they're a great resource for talking through these options.

And if you don't? You can always schedule time at BrickhouseAgency.com, the boutique Medicare agency run by my wife, Niki. She and her team work with people across the country to help them make informed Medicare decisions – whether it's evaluating a potential switch or simply understanding the pros and cons more clearly.

Matt Tip: This isn't just about math – it's about you.

If you've ever had a major illness – like cancer, heart disease, or even a big surgery – those things don't just vanish from your record. They shape what might happen next.

And if you've got a strong family history of chronic illness – diabetes, Parkinson's, strokes,

Alzheimer's, you name it – don't assume you'll coast through Medicare with minimal care.

Medigap might feel expensive today. But if your health changes and you want to switch later, you might not be allowed to.

This is the kind of decision that's easy to skip over when you're feeling healthy, but it's exactly when you should think it through.

THE DECISION GUIDE: WHICH PATH FITS YOU BEST?

This section isn't a worksheet. It's a moment to pause, reflect, and think clearly about the kind of coverage that actually fits your life.

Both Medicare Supplement (Medigap) and Medicare Advantage (MAPD) plans have their place. But only one is likely to work best for you, and this will help you figure out which.

IF YOU ANSWER YES TO MOST OF THESE QUESTIONS, MEDIGAP MIGHT BE THE RIGHT FIT

- ✅ Do you want to be able to see any doctor who takes Medicare, without worrying about networks?

- ✅ Do you travel or live part of the year in another state?

- ✓ Would you rather pay more in monthly premiums to avoid surprise bills later?

- ✓ Are you concerned about getting denied if you want to switch plans in the future?

- ✓ Do you value stability and predictability over built-in extras?

Matt Tip: If you answered yes to three or more of these, it's worth taking a serious look at Medigap, especially if you're still in your open enrollment period and can qualify without medical underwriting.

IF YOU ANSWER YES TO MOST OF THESE QUESTIONS, MAPD MIGHT BE A BETTER FIT

- ✓ Do you want lower monthly premiums and don't mind copays or networks?

- ✓ Do you like having dental, vision, or hearing benefits built into one plan?

- ✓ Are all your preferred doctors and hospitals in-network – and likely to stay there?

- ✓ Do you rarely need specialist care or frequent medical treatment?

✅ Are you comfortable following preapproval rules and reading the fine print?

Matt Tip: MAPD can work great for healthy people with low usage – but the tradeoff is control. Make sure you're comfortable with the plan's rules and limits before you enroll.

5 REASONS PEOPLE REGRET CHOOSING MEDICARE ADVANTAGE

1. They didn't realize how narrow the network was until they needed a specialist.

2. They assumed the plan would cover major hospitals or cancer centers – but it didn't.

3. They underestimated the true out-of-pocket costs for frequent care.

4. They thought they could switch to Medigap later but couldn't pass underwriting.

5. They chose based on a TV ad – not what actually matched their life.

Of course, Medigap has its own drawbacks. It's not all sunshine and no copays.

5 REASONS PEOPLE REGRET CHOOSING MEDICARE SUPPLEMENT

1. They didn't realize premiums rise every year with age and inflation.

2. They forgot that Medigap doesn't include drug coverage.

3. They thought "no networks" meant any doctor, anytime.

4. They paid high premiums but barely used any care.

5. They bought from a big-name carrier without shopping around.

Matt Tip: You don't get do-overs in Medicare. If you're going MAPD, go in eyes wide open. If you're leaning Medigap, this might be your only shot.

PLANNING AHEAD: 3 WAYS TO SET YOURSELF UP FOR FEWER MEDICARE SURPRISES

1. **Know your enrollment windows.** Your Medigap Open Enrollment Period may be the only time you can enroll without answering health questions. Mark it on your calendar.

2. **Think long-term, not just today.** Are you healthy now? Great. What happens if that changes? Will you still be happy with your choice?

3. **Evaluate where you'll live, travel, or spend time.** MAPD plans are county-specific. If your lifestyle spans regions, Medigap may be worth the premium.

Want to go deeper on this? My full courses, books, articles and a ton of free Helpful Links are at PrepareforMedicare.com and walk through these tradeoffs in detail.

CHAPTER 6

HOW TO DECIDE
WHAT'S RIGHT FOR YOU

If Chapter 5 laid out the math, this one gets personal. Because Medicare isn't just a numbers game – it's about how you live, where you go, what kind of care you'll need, and how you feel about risk.

You've made it this far, and that means you're doing the work. You're asking smart questions, comparing options, and thinking ahead. That alone puts you way ahead of most people navigating Medicare.

But now we're at the heart of it:

"So… which one should I pick?"

This is the most common question I get – from individuals, couples, and even professionals who refer clients to my materials and courses. And while I'll never tell you what to do, I *will* give you a decision-making framework that helps you arrive at the right choice for you – backed by decades of experience from inside the Medicare industry.

In this chapter, we'll walk through:

- ✅ Key questions to ask yourself

- ✅ How to weigh cost vs. risk vs. lifestyle

- ✅ Common profiles that lean toward Medigap or MAPD

- ✅ What to do if you're still not sure

FIRST: YOUR STARTING POINT MATTERS

Are you just turning 65? Still working and delaying Medicare? On a retiree plan and wondering if it's time to switch?

Where you are in your Medicare journey affects your options – and your flexibility.

If you're brand new to Medicare, you likely have guaranteed issue rights to get a Medigap plan without answering health questions. That's a one-time window (unless you live in certain states), and once it closes, switching later gets harder.

If you're coming off an employer plan or COBRA, your options depend on the timing of your enrollment. That's why it's crucial to have your timeline right.

YOUR BUDGET VS. YOUR RISK TOLERANCE

Some people simply can't afford the monthly premiums of a Medigap plan + Part D. That's not a knock – it's reality.

But others *can* afford it – they just don't want to pay more unless it's clearly worth it. That's where understanding your risk tolerance comes into play.

Ask yourself:

- ✅ Would I rather pay a predictable amount every month – even if I rarely use it?

- ✅ Or would I rather roll the dice with lower monthly costs, even if it might cost more down the road?

There's no right answer. But it's a deeply personal one.

YOUR LIFESTYLE AND PREFERENCES

This might be the biggest one – and the most overlooked.

Do you:

- ✅ Travel frequently across state lines?

- ✅ Have multiple residences or move seasonally?

- ✅ Want to keep your same doctors, no matter what?

- ✅ Hate jumping through hoops for care?

If you answered yes to any of those, a Medigap plan may give you peace of mind that's worth the higher premium.

On the other hand:

- ✅ Are you comfortable with managed care?

- ✅ Do you like the idea of dental, vision, or fitness perks built in?

- ✅ Would you rather keep premiums low and pay only when you use care?

Then an MAPD plan might fit your style – and your budget – just fine.

WHERE YOU LIVE MATTERS, TOO

One thing most people overlook when comparing plans? Your ZIP Code doesn't tell the whole story – but your county does.

Medicare Advantage plans are approved at the county level, not state-wide or nationwide. That means plan availability and quality can vary a lot depending on where you live.

- ✓ In major metro areas, there are usually plenty of MAPD options – some with strong networks, added benefits, and competitive star ratings.

- ✓ In suburban areas, you may still have good choices, but the networks might be narrower or benefits less generous.

- ✓ In rural counties, plan options are often limited – or nonexistent. Even if a plan is technically available, the provider network may be so small it's not usable for real care.

This is one reason two people with similar needs can make totally different Medicare choices – simply based on geography. Medigap plans offer more consistency across states, but Medicare Advantage is very local.

Matt Tip: You're not just choosing an insurance plan. You're choosing how you want to experience healthcare in retirement.

Earlier in the book, you walked through some key questions to help decide which path fits you best – Medigap or MAPD. If you haven't already done that, flip back to Chapter 5 and take a moment.

But now that you've seen the deeper trade-offs – cost, risk, access, service, geography – here's a **quick recap** to help clarify your direction.

MEDIGAP MIGHT BE RIGHT FOR YOU IF:

- ✅ You want freedom to see any doctor who takes Medicare, anywhere in the U.S.

- ✅ You don't want to deal with referrals or preapprovals

- ✅ You prefer paying more monthly in exchange for fewer billing surprises

- ✅ You're entering Medicare and want to lock in guaranteed coverage without medical underwriting

- ✅ You value long-term stability over built-in perks

MAPD MIGHT BE RIGHT FOR YOU IF:

- ✅ You want a low (or $0) premium and don't mind cost-sharing

- ✅ You're comfortable using a provider network

- ✅ You like the convenience of drug, dental, and vision all in one plan

- ✅ Your doctors and hospitals are in-network and likely to stay

- ✅ You're okay reviewing and possibly switching plans each year

There's no right answer – only the right answer *for you*. And now, you've got the tools to make it.

PROFILES IN CHOICE

LET'S BRING THIS TO LIFE WITH A FEW EXAMPLES:

Janet, 67: Retired teacher, loves to travel

She splits time between Florida and Michigan. She sees specialists in both states. Janet chooses Medigap Plan G because she values flexibility and doesn't want to worry about networks.

Carlos and Maria, 65: Budget-conscious couple

They're both in good health, live in a metro area with strong MAPD options, and want to keep costs down. They pick an MAPD plan with a $0 premium and decent dental coverage.

Derek, 70: Cancer survivor.

He's been in remission for five years. He starts on a MAPD plan but gets denied Medigap coverage when trying to switch later. He now wishes he'd started with Medigap when he had the chance.

Cindy, 68: HR exec, still working

She's delaying Part B and only has Part A for now. When she retires next year, she plans to work with an independent agent to shop both Medigap and MAPD options.

These aren't theoretical. These are real-world stories I've heard and helped solve over and over again.

If You're Still Not Sure…

That's okay.

Choosing between Medigap and MAPD isn't a quick decision – and it shouldn't be. You don't have to rush. And you don't have to do it alone.

This is where working with a licensed, independent Medicare insurance agent really helps. Someone who represents multiple companies – not just one – and who can walk you through the pros and cons based on your actual ZIP Code and situation.

If you don't have one of those, again – my wife Niki's firm (Brickhouse Agency) has a whole team of them. You'll find more at <u>BrickhouseAgency.com</u>, or by starting at <u>PrepareforMedicare.com</u> .

Matt Tip: If an agent only shows you one plan – or only one company's plans – you're not working with an advisor. You're working with a salesperson.

In Summary

This chapter wasn't meant to give you *the* answer.

It was meant to help you find *your* answer.

Because the truth is, both Medigap and MAPD can work beautifully – for the right person, in the right situation.

Your job is to:

- ✔ Understand what matters to you
- ✔ Understand how each path delivers (or doesn't)
- ✔ Be honest about your health, habits, and goals

And my job is to help light the path so you don't get lost.

In the final chapter, we'll wrap it all up – and make sure you leave this book with clarity, confidence, and a plan.

Matt Tip: The right Medicare decision isn't just smart. It's personal. And now you're ready to make it.

STRATEGIC INSIGHTS

WHAT MOST PEOPLE NEVER HEAR ABOUT MEDICARE ADVANTAGE

This isn't about scaring you. It's about equipping you with the same context I wish every consumer had before they picked a Medicare Advantage plan, especially one they might later regret.

MEDICARE ADVANTAGE IS A GOVERNMENT OUTSOURCING PROGRAM, AND THAT CHANGES THE GAME

When you sign up for a Medicare Advantage plan (MAPD), you're not just picking a new insurance company, you're shifting how your Medicare benefits are administered.

Instead of the federal government paying providers directly, Medicare pays a private insurance company to manage your care. That company now calls the shots.

- ✅ They control the rules for approvals, networks, and cost-sharing.

✅ They're paid a flat rate per member – so the fewer services you use, the more they keep.

✅ Their incentives are different than Original Medicare's.

This structure isn't automatically bad – but it's rarely explained clearly.

Matt Tip: When an insurance company runs your Medicare, their job is to keep you healthy and profitable. That creates trade-offs – especially when care gets expensive.

MID-YEAR NETWORK CHANGES CAN HAPPEN

Yes, your MAPD plan can change its provider network **in the middle of the year** – and it happens more often than people expect.

✅ You'll get 30 days' notice if a doctor or hospital leaves your network.

✅ You may lose access to specialists or facilities you counted on.

✅ Unless CMS grants a Special Enrollment Period (SEP), **you won't be able to change plans** just because your doctor is no longer in-network.

Some people find out too late – and must wait until the Annual Election Period to make a change.

Matt Tip: MAPD networks aren't permanent. That top-rated hospital today might be out tomorrow – and you might not have a backup plan.

WHY YOUR CALL TO CUSTOMER SERVICE MIGHT NOT HELP

Many MAPD members are shocked at how little help they get when something goes wrong. Here's why:

- ✓ The plan may outsource customer service to a third-party vendor.

- ✓ Claims, pharmacy benefits, and prior authorizations may all be managed by different vendors – not the plan itself.

- ✓ The rep on the phone might not have access to the full picture – or the authority to solve anything.

This fragmentation can make even simple issues hard to resolve. And when the stakes are high – like during a cancer diagnosis or a surgery delay – it gets real, fast.

Matt Tip: A "good" plan on paper doesn't mean good support when things go sideways. And when you're in pain or panicked, the last thing you want is finger-pointing between vendors.

MEDICARE STAR RATINGS: NOT WHAT YOU THINK

Star Ratings are widely used in ads and brochures – but here's what most people don't realize:

- ✅ Star Ratings are based on performance from two years ago, not last year.

- ✅ Plans with 4 or 5 stars can still drop dramatically if performance slides – but that change won't show up right away.

- ✅ Some new or regional plans can start strong, but falter as they scale.

Star Ratings measure some important things – like preventive care and call center response times – but they don't measure your local hospital access, billing accuracy, or how easy it is to get a real person on the phone.

Matt Tip: Star Ratings tell you something – but not everything. Don't assume a "5-Star" plan is bulletproof.

WHAT TO ACTUALLY LOOK FOR BEHIND THE SCENES

When comparing MAPD plans, dig deeper than the brochure. Ask:

- ✓ Does the company have deep experience managing Medicare – not just commercial insurance?

- ✓ Do they run customer service and care coordination in-house – or do they outsource?

- ✓ What's their recent history with provider networks and hospital terminations?

- ✓ Do they invest in infrastructure – or just sales?

These aren't always easy questions to answer – but they're the ones that matter when you're relying on a plan to manage your health.

If you want help evaluating carriers from the inside out, make sure to check out the Bonus Chapter: *How to Read an Insurance Company (Like an Insider).*

CHAPTER 7

FINAL THOUGHTS AND WHAT TO DO NEXT

You made it to the end – and I hope you're feeling more confident than when you started.

Let's recap what you've just done:

- ✓ You reviewed how Original Medicare works – and where it doesn't.

- ✓ You explored the strengths and weaknesses of Medigap and MAPD plans.

- ✓ You saw real-life examples, real costs, and real consequences.

- ✓ You got a step-by-step framework for making a smart, personalized choice.

You didn't need a sales pitch. Just the truth, from someone who's been deep inside the system for over 20 years and who's helped thousands of people navigate this exact same decision.

So, what now?

Here's how to take your next steps:

1. Revisit Your Notes

- ✅ Go back through your highlights, bookmarks, and gut reactions. Did anything surprise you? Did anything jump out as a dealbreaker – or a must-have?

- ✅ Your instincts are usually right. Pay attention to them.

2. Talk With an Independent Agent

- ✅ This book was never about selling you insurance – it was about helping you understand what matters, why it matters, and what to do about it.

That said, the next step should be a conversation with a licensed, experienced, independent Medicare insurance agent. Someone who can show you multiple options. Someone who isn't tied to one carrier. Someone who knows your ZIP Code.

I know I've mentioned this before, but it's worth repeating: I'm a big fan of independent Medicare insurance agents. Always have been. I've trained them, worked alongside them, and built programs to support them. They do hard, important work – and when you find a good one, they're worth their weight in gold.

If you don't know where to turn, my wife Niki runs a boutique agency called The Brickhouse Agency. Her team works in nearly every state and helps people just like you every day.

You can:

- ✓ Visit BrickhouseAgency.com

- ✓ Schedule a no-pressure consultation (phone or Zoom)

- ✓ Learn more at PrepareforMedicare.com

Whether you talk to Niki's team or not, promise me this: don't make this decision in the dark.

3. If You're Turning 65 Soon

- ✓ Mark your calendar for your Initial Enrollment Period (IEP): it starts 3 months before, includes your birth month, and ends 3 months after

- ✓ Use this time to evaluate your needs and compare plan options

- ✓ Don't wait until the last minute – Medicare is too important

4. If You're Already Enrolled in Medicare

- ✓ Review your coverage every year – especially during the Annual Election Period (AEP), October 15 to December 7

- ✓ Read your Annual Notice of Change (ANOC) from your insurance plan – don't ignore it

- ✓ If you're not happy with your coverage, switch. You're not locked in forever (unless you waited too long for Medigap)

5. Take Action Before Your Enrollment Deadline

- ✓ If you're new to Medicare, you only get one Medigap Open Enrollment Period – and it doesn't come back. Use it wisely.

- ✓ If you're reviewing coverage during AEP, don't procrastinate. Benefits change, networks shift, and the sooner you act, the more control you have.

☑ If you're still working or delaying Medicare, start gathering your facts and laying the groundwork now.

Matt Tip: Medicare isn't one decision. It's a series of them. Start strong, and you'll avoid the biggest regrets.

In Closing…

Medicare isn't fun. It isn't flashy. And it's rarely simple.

But it's important. It touches your money, your health, and your peace of mind.

And now – you're ready.

Thanks for reading. Thanks for thinking. And thanks for taking control of this part of your life. You're making a smart move.

Still wondering which insurance company to trust – or how to spot the ones that talk a big game but don't deliver?

I've added a Bonus Chapter right after this one called *"How to Read an Insurance Company (Like an Insider)."*

It's where I pull back the curtain on how Medicare carriers actually operate – and give you the tools to separate the pros from the pretenders. If you've ever wondered what really goes on behind the scenes... that's where I spill the good stuff.

WANT MORE RESOURCES?

If this book helped, there's more where that came from.

I've built a full library of tools, guides, and real-world advice to help you navigate Medicare, Social Security, and retirement – without the jargon, the runaround, or the pressure.

You'll find:

- Medicare video courses and checklists

- The Matt Feret Newsletter

- A booking link to for a free, no-obligation Medicare Consultation from Niki's Brickhouse Agency staff

- The full Prepare for Medicare® book and workbook

- A trusted referral path for Social Security guidance

- A trusted referral path for IRMAA guidance

- Interviews and insights on aging, money, healthcare, and life after 50

All available at:

PrepareforMedicare.com

PrepareforSocialSecurity.com

TheMattFeretShow.com

No gimmicks. No hype. Just honest, experienced guidance from someone who's been inside the system – so you don't have to figure it out alone.

And if you're on social media, follow me on LinkedIn, Facebook, or YouTube – where I post new tips, interviews, and updates weekly.

Until next time –

Here's to your Wealth, Wisdom and Wellness!

—matt feret

Author, Advocate, Longtime Medicare Industry Executive, and Medicare Nerd

HOW TO READ
AN INSURANCE COMPANY
(LIKE AN INSIDER)

This chapter is based on my personal observations and professional experience working across a range of Medicare insurance carriers. These are my opinions alone – not affiliated with any current or former employer.

Let's say you've narrowed your choice to a Medigap or MAPD plan – but now you're staring at a bunch of logos, wondering…

"Which insurance company should I choose?"

Here's what most people don't realize: not all Medicare insurance companies are created equal.

Some are huge national players. Others are tiny regionals. Some have decades of experience and deep Medicare infrastructure. Others? Not so much.

And as someone who's spent more than two decades inside this industry – working for national carriers, multi-state regionals, and state-based Medicare plans, I've seen it all. Let me tell you – who's running the show matters.

COMPANY SIZE: BIGGER IS (USUALLY) BETTER

If a company doesn't have at least 100,000 people enrolled in its Medicare Supplement plans? Red flag. Doesn't have at least 100,000 enrolled in its Medicare Advantage plans? Red flag.

Why? Because size = revenue. And revenue = investment.

If they're not making real money on the product, they're not going to:

- ✅ Hire experienced Medicare leadership

- ✅ Build good infrastructure

- ✅ Invest in customer service, networks, or innovation

That means they're likely outsourcing most of it – and doing just enough to play in the space. My opinion? That's risky.

THE TALENT GAP IS REAL

At one company I worked with, there was one person in charge of Medicare data and analytics. At a large national carrier I worked for, there were eighty. That's not just a headcount difference – it's a signal of how seriously the company takes Medicare.

Many small or new Medicare insurance companies don't have the right people in place. Their network team might be inexperienced, their finance team may not fully understand Medicare risk adjustment, and their actuarial team may have little or no Medicare-specific experience – so, you guessed it, they outsource that work to one of many consulting firms that specialize in Medicare pricing and forecasting. Even their at-home visit programs could be managed by outside vendors with little oversight.

When this happens, plans often struggle financially. And when they do? They either:

- Pull out of counties
- Reduce benefits
- Or quietly degrade service and support

This especially matters for MAPD plans. If a plan is under pressure, it can show up in:

- ✔ Narrowing networks

- ✔ Fewer perks

- ✔ Increased denials

- ✔ Or a drop in their Medicare Star Ratings

NOT ALL SMALL PLANS ARE BAD

Some smaller, regional Medicare Advantage plans are excellent. They know their market, have tight provider relationships, and may even offer better customer service than the big guys and gals.

The key is to look at trends:

- ✔ Has the plan been improving its Star Ratings – or are they falling?

- ✔ Are they expanding into new ZIP Codes – or are they exiting markets?

Unfortunately, Medicare.gov doesn't show you a Star Rating trend over time – just the current year. But a quick internet search (or asking your agent) may reveal more than you'd expect.

Try searching for the plan name + "Medicare Star Rating history" or check local news or business journals for hospital system disputes or exits. You'll often find useful breadcrumbs.

VENDOR OVERLOAD

Many small plans don't "*do*" Medicare – they outsource Medicare. Sure, their name may be on the card, but that's about it. What do I mean?

The provider network? Managed by a vendor. Risk adjustment? Vendor. Customer service? Vendor.

Even the people managing the vendors may be junior, overworked, or spread thin. And the vendors don't treat these plans like VIP clients, because… they're not.

This lack of internal expertise leads to missed deadlines, poor performance, and – you guessed it – trouble for members.

LEADERSHIP MATTERS

Does the CEO have experience running a health insurance company – or did they come from outside the industry? Is the Chief Medical Officer experienced in Medicare Advantage programs? Does the compliance team understand CMS regulations inside and out? Who's leading the provider contracting team – and do they have the credibility to negotiate effectively? Many insurance companies have deleted their leadership bios from their webpages due to security reasons. But if you dig deep enough, you can find what you need to know.

These roles matter more than most people think. The best-run plans are led by people who've lived and breathed Medicare – or at the very least, understand the health insurance industry from the inside out. If the top leadership team has very little prior experience running an insurance company, that's a red flag. Medicare isn't something you can learn on the fly – it takes years to understand how the system works, how plans succeed or fail, and how to deliver long-term value to members.

And this is where large, national companies – or regional carriers that prioritize Medicare as a major line of business – often have an advantage. When Medicare makes up a significant percentage of their revenue or membership, they naturally attract and retain leaders with deep Medicare knowledge. Their internal culture reflects that priority.

Smaller carriers, especially those with roots in commercial insurance or life insurance, may treat Medicare as a "side business." When that happens, the leadership team may lack Medicare-specific experience altogether. It's not uncommon to find executives steering Medicare strategy who've never worked in the space before. That's not just a learning curve – that's a liability. Medicare is too important to be treated as an add-on or secondary business line. You want a leadership team that understands its complexity – and makes it a priority.

And here's another piece that gets overlooked: the HR leader. Just like other leadership roles, you want to know: does the head of HR – and their team – have any Medicare or health insurance experience? What's their background? If they've never hired for Medicare roles before, that's a problem.

Finding Medicare-experienced professionals is difficult. There aren't that many of us, and the ones who are good at it? Already working elsewhere. If the HR team doesn't know what to look for – or can't find or attract top-tier talent – you end up with a weak bench, shallow leadership, and teams that don't know what they don't know.

And if executives don't know what great Medicare insurance professional look like, they may not recognize poor performance either. That leads to underperformance quietly persisting and missed opportunities to improve plan operations or member experience.

A company dedicated to Medicare invests in leadership and the people behind the scenes. They prioritize hiring experts, not just warm bodies or vendors. They know that getting Medicare right is hard – and they treat it like the specialized field it is.

You won't find these details in the plan brochure. So, dig. Look up the company's About Us page. Scan for executive bios. Check Crain's, Becker's, or your local business journal. Snoop around LinkedIn. If the leadership team has little or no health insurance background – or their Medicare department is a revolving door and looks cobbled together overnight, that's worth knowing.

You want to be with a Medicare insurance carrier that's playing to win – not just dabbling in Medicare to see if it works.

"A leader is one who knows the way, goes the way, and shows the way."

– John C. Maxwell

That's especially true in Medicare.

If the people running your plan don't know the system – haven't worked in it, don't understand it, or treat it like a side project – you'll be the one who pays for their learning curve. In service delays. In shrinking networks. In benefit cuts.

I've seen firsthand what happens when executives with zero Medicare experience try to "figure it out on the fly." It doesn't end well – for the members.

Questions to Research:

If you're the type who really likes to dig in, here are a few more pro-level questions to explore:

- ✅ What percentage of the company's overall revenue comes from Medicare products? If it's low, Medicare may be an afterthought. If it's high – or even their top line of business – that's a sign they're likely to invest heavily in the people, systems, and support Medicare members actually need.

- ✅ How many years have they been in the Medicare Advantage business? Were they part of the re-launch after the Medicare Modernization Act of 2003 (for the 2005/2006 plan year)? Or did they just get into the game recently?

- ✓ Have they ever exited the Medicare market in a county or state – only to come back later? That could signal inconsistency or financial instability.

When comparing insurance companies, especially smaller ones – ask:

- ✓ How many Medicare members do they have nationally? In your state?

- ✓ What's their Star Rating? What's the Star Rating been over the last 3-5 years?

- ✓ Have they entered or exited your county in the last 5 years?

- ✓ Is their Medicare health plan membership growing or shrinking?

- ✓ How big is their provider network? Is it growing, or shrinking?

And if you can, search their name alongside terms like "contract dispute" or "hospital system exit." You might be surprised by what you find in local news.

FINAL THOUGHT

Choosing a plan isn't just about which plan. It's about who's behind it.

You wouldn't buy a car from a company that just started building them last year. Don't buy your Medicare plan that way, either.

And while much of this chapter is based on my own experience and point of view, I share it to help you think critically – not to hand you a one-size-fits-all answer. Ask questions. Compare options. And don't be afraid to lean on a trusted advisor to help you sort through it all.

Matt Tip: An insurance company is only as good as its leadership, its experience, and its ability to invest in the product. You deserve one that takes Medicare seriously.

FREQUENTLY ASKED QUESTIONS

MEDICARE SUPPLEMENT VS. MEDICARE ADVANTAGE

You've read the book, but you may still have lingering questions. That's normal – and smart. Here are some of the most common questions I get, along with real answers from someone who spent 20+ years on the inside.

Matt Tip: Learning the language of Medicare gives you power. If you understand the terms, you'll understand the choices.

1. **What's the biggest mistake people make when choosing between Medigap and Medicare Advantage?**

   Waiting too long to figure it out.

Your best chance to get a Medigap plan with no health questions is when you first go on Medicare Part B. If you miss that window, you may lose your ability to get one later – especially if your health changes. Too many people wait until something bad happens, then realize they can't switch. That's the mistake you want to avoid.

2. **Is Medigap always more expensive?**

On a monthly basis, yes. But over time? Not always.

Medigap plans have higher premiums, but lower out-of-pocket costs when you use medical services. MAPD plans often have $0 premiums, but you'll often pay more as you use services. If you have a rough year – or several – it adds up fast. I walk through this math in Chapter 5.

3. **Do Medigap plans cover dental, vision, or hearing?**

Nope. Medigap only covers what Original Medicare covers – plus most of what Medicare leaves behind like coinsurance and deductibles. You'll need to buy separate stand-alone plans for dental, vision, and hearing. Many people buy those through the same agent who helps them with their Medigap plan.

4. What about Part B giveback plans? Are they worth it?

Maybe. My opinion? Probably not.

These are MAPD plans that advertise something like "Get $100 back on your Social Security check!" Sounds good, right? But you've got to read the fine print.

Most giveback plans reduce your Part B premium but also reduce your benefits. That lower cost comes with fewer bells and whistles – or tighter networks. Sometimes both. It's a tradeoff, not a bonus.

5. Can I switch between Medigap and MAPD every year?

Sort of. But not the way you think.

You can switch MAPD plans every year during AEP (October 15 – December 7). You've got the MA-OEP from January 1 to March 31, too. And, if you have a Medigap plan, you can use the AEP to switch to a MAPD plan. But if you want to switch from MAPD to Medigap, you'll usually have to pass medical underwriting – unless you qualify for a special guaranteed issue right.

So yes, you can apply to switch. But no, it's not always approved.

6. **What's the difference between a PPO and an HMO MAPD plan?**

It's all about network flexibility.

- ✅ HMO plans usually require you to stay in-network and get referrals.

- ✅ PPO plans let you go out-of-network, but often at higher costs.

Many people think PPOs give you "freedom," but that freedom can get expensive, fast. And just because a provider is listed as "in network" doesn't mean they'll take the plan – or have appointments available. Provider directories, even online ones, are usually chock-full of errors and are outdated.

7. **What if my doctors or hospital stop accepting my MAPD plan?**

It happens more than you think.

As I mention (a lot!), provider directories are often outdated or wrong. Worse, hospitals and large systems have been cutting ties with MAPD plans more frequently. You might even get a letter in the mail saying your doctor is dropping your plan – or read about it in the newspaper.

If you're in the middle of treatment or have something scheduled, it can be disruptive, stressful, and expensive. This doesn't happen with Medigap. As long as the provider accepts Medicare, you're covered.

8.   What's a MOOP, and why does it matter?

MOOP = Maximum Out-of-Pocket.

Every MAPD plan has one. It's the most you'll pay for covered medical services in a year. Some MOOPs are as low as $3,000. Others go beyond $8,000. If you have an out-of-network feature on your MAPD plan (PPO, some HMOs), those MOOPs can go into the five-figure range. Annually.

Important: The MOOP only applies to the medical portion of your plan – not your prescription drugs (Part D). Your drug spending has its own set of thresholds and caps.

This number matters because if you hit it, that's how much you've paid – on top of your premium. Understanding your plan's MOOP is essential. It's your worst-case scenario for medical expenses under your MAPD plan.

9. **Can my MAPD or Part D plan change every year?**

    Yes – and they often do. In fact, I can't recall a single plan that didn't change every year.

    Your monthly premium, drug coverage, network, and benefits can change annually. That's why you get the Annual Notice of Change (ANOC) in the mail every fall. Read it!

    Your plan might drop your doctors, raise your copays, or stop covering one of your meds. One of the reasons the Annual Enrollment Period (October 15 – December 7) exists because plans change.

10. **Do I really need to work with an insurance agent?**

    No. But it helps.

    You *can* do this yourself on Medicare. gov – but be warned. That site doesn't show provider networks for MAPD plans, doesn't account for preferred pharmacies, and often lacks clarity. I cover these "Frustrating Flaws" of Medicare.gov in my flagship book, *Prepare for Medicare – The Insider's Guide to Buying Medicare Insurance* and in my flagship course, *The Prepare for Medicare Mini-Course* at length.

A licensed, independent Medicare insurance agent can:

- ✅ Help you compare plans in your ZIP Code

- ✅ Show you behind-the-scenes differences you won't find online

- ✅ Save you time, frustration, and possibly money

If you've got a great agent already – awesome. Stick with them. If you don't, I'll remind you yet again my wife Niki and her team at Brickhouse Agency can help. No pressure. Just clarity.

11. Can I use a Medicare Advantage plan while traveling out of state?

It depends on your plan. HMO plans typically only cover emergency or urgent care outside your service area. PPO plans often allow out-of-network care – but with a separate deductible and higher coinsurance (sometimes 40–50%). If you regularly live in more than one state or travel for extended periods, Medigap is often the more flexible option.

12. Why do Medigap Plan G premiums vary so much between companies?

Because the price reflects more than the benefits – it reflects how the insurance company manages risk. While Plan G benefits are standardized, pricing depends on things like **medical loss ratio (MLR)** and how the company structures its risk pool. MLR refers to how much of your premium the company spends on actual claims. Some companies open a block of policies, and if not enough healthy people join, that block becomes more expensive over time. Others close old blocks and open new ones to attract healthier enrollees – leaving the old block to age and face bigger rate hikes. Not every agent explains this. Many don't know. That's why choosing a Medigap carrier with the right structure – and with help from someone who understands this – is just as important as choosing the right plan letter.

13. How does the 12-month Trial Right work – and who qualifies?

You qualify the **first time you join a Medicare Advantage (MAPD) plan** – regardless of age. You might be 65, 67, or 75. If it's your first time on an MAPD plan, you get a one-time, 12-month window to change your mind. During that time, you can switch back to Original Medicare and enroll in a Medigap plan without answering health questions. But once those 12 months pass, the window closes for good.

14. If I'm healthy now, does it really make sense to choose Medigap?

It might. Because if your health changes and you want to switch into Medigap later, you may have to go through medical underwriting. You could be denied or charged more based on your age and conditions. Medigap gives you flexibility and predictability, and the best time to qualify is when you're healthy.

15. What is a Part B giveback plan – and is it worth it?

These MAPD plans reduce the amount of your Part B premium that's taken out of your Social Security check. It can sound like "free money," but the tradeoff may come in other areas: fewer benefits, tighter networks, or higher drug or medical costs. Make sure the rest of the plan still works for your needs.

16. If my spouse becomes eligible for Medicare after I do, do I need to change my plan?

No. Medicare is individual coverage. You each make your own decision. That said, if you both enroll in MAPD plans, it's worth checking that your doctors are in both networks – and your costs and benefits line up the way you expect.

17. Do call centers only represent a few plans?

Most large call centers represent many Medicare Advantage carriers – but they're trained to lead with specific plans. Some emphasize products that are simpler to explain, or where they've had high enrollments. Others may follow a scripted approach. That doesn't mean the reps are doing anything wrong – it just means you may not get the full picture unless you ask for it. If you want more customized guidance, consider working with an independent advisor who isn't bound by those call flows.

18. Do MAPD plans cover top hospitals and cancer centers?

Not always. Some high-profile hospitals and cancer centers don't participate in certain MAPD plan networks. Just because the plan has a big name doesn't mean every facility is in. If access to a specific provider matters to you, always check – and double-check – network participation before you enroll. Call the provider and check, and be ready to be very specific about which type of coverage, the plan number, plan type and carrier you've got. Don't just ask, "Do you accept (Company Name)?"

19. What's the difference between deductibles and MOOP in Medicare Advantage?

MAPD plans often have two separate deductibles: one for medical services (like hospital care or outpatient visits), and one for prescription drugs. The **Maximum Out-of-Pocket (MOOP)** applies only to the medical portion of the plan – not the drug side. That means you could hit your MOOP and still pay ongoing costs for medications. Many people confuse this – and assume everything is capped. It's not.

20. Can I just pick the plan with the lowest monthly premium?

You can – but the lowest premium doesn't mean lowest cost. You could face higher copays, more restrictions, or higher out-of-pocket spending over time. Always look at the full package – benefits, flexibility, and total expected costs – before deciding.

Matt Tip: If you still have questions after reading this FAQ, that's a good sign. You're thinking critically – and you're going to make a smart decision.

GLOSSARY OF MEDICARE TERMS

This glossary includes the most important terms you'll encounter as you compare Medicare Supplement and Medicare Advantage plans. The goal here isn't to overwhelm you, it's to help you feel confident using the language you'll hear from insurance companies, agents, and even friends.

Annual Election Period (AEP)
The window from October 15 to December 7 each year when you can switch Medicare Advantage or Part D plans. This does not apply to Medigap.

Annual Notice of Change (ANOC)
A letter your Medicare Advantage or Part D plan sends you each fall that outlines what's changing next year – premiums, benefits, drugs covered, etc. Always read this.

Coinsurance

A percentage of the cost you pay for a healthcare service. For example, you might pay 20% of a doctor visit charge under Original Medicare.

Copayment (Copay)

A fixed amount you pay for a service, like $10 for a doctor visit or $35 for a specialist.

Deductible

The amount you must pay out-of-pocket before your Medicare coverage (or drug plan) begins paying.

Formulary

A list of prescription drugs covered by a Part D or MAPD plan. Drugs are grouped into tiers – lower tiers are cheaper, higher tiers cost more.

General Enrollment Period (GEP)

If you didn't sign up for Medicare Part B when you were first eligible and aren't eligible for a Special Enrollment Period, you can enroll between January 1 and March 31 each year. Your coverage begins the month after you enroll.

Guaranteed Issue

A right to enroll in a Medigap plan without health questions or medical underwriting. Most people get this when they first enroll in Medicare Part B.

Initial Coverage Election Period (ICEP)

Your first opportunity to enroll in a Medicare Advantage (MAPD) plan. It usually lines up with your Initial Enrollment Period unless you delay enrolling in Part B.

Initial Enrollment Period (IEP)

Your first chance to enroll in Medicare – 3 months before, the month of, and 3 months after your 65th birthday (or Part B eligibility). This applies to Part A, Part B, and Part D.

Medicare Advantage (MAPD)

A private insurance plan that combines Medicare Part A, Part B, and usually Part D. It may include extra benefits like dental or vision. Often has networks, referrals, and copays.

Medicare.gov

The official U.S. government site for Medicare information and enrollment. Useful, but limited – especially for comparing Medicare Advantage networks and Medigap plans.

Medicare Supplement (Medigap)

Insurance that fills the "gaps" in Original Medicare, like deductibles, coinsurance, and copayments. You must have both Medicare Part A and Part B to enroll.

MOOP (Maximum Out-of-Pocket)

The most you'll pay out-of-pocket for medical services under a MAPD plan in a calendar year. Does not include prescription drug costs.

Network

The group of doctors, hospitals, and providers contracted with a Medicare Advantage plan. Medigap plans do not have networks – as long as the provider accepts Medicare.

Open Enrollment Period (OEP)

There are two common uses for this term. The first refers to your **Medigap Open Enrollment Period** – the six months after you enroll in Medicare Part B when you can get any Medigap plan without medical underwriting. The second is the **Medicare Advantage Open Enrollment Period (MA-OEP)**, which runs from January 1 to March 31 each year. During the MA-OEP, you can switch from one MAPD plan to another or drop your MAPD plan and return to Original Medicare with or without a Part D plan. Special rules apply – this period is only for people already enrolled in a Medicare Advantage plan as of January 1.

Out-of-Pocket Maximum

Same as MOOP. The cap on what you'll pay for covered medical care in a MAPD plan before the plan covers 100%.

Part A

Original Medicare hospital insurance. Covers inpatient care, skilled nursing, and limited home health care.

Part B

Original Medicare medical insurance. Covers doctor visits, outpatient care, and preventive services. It has a monthly premium.

Part C

Medicare Advantage

Part D

Prescription drug coverage. Can be included in a MAPD plan or purchased separately if you have a Medigap plan.

Premium

The amount you pay monthly for a Medicare plan. Medigap premiums are usually higher than MAPD premiums.

Prior Authorization

Approval required before receiving certain tests, procedures, or prescriptions – common in MAPD plans, not in Medigap.

Referral

Permission from your primary care doctor to see a specialist. Often required in HMO-style MAPD plans.

Underwriting

A health screening process to assess current and likely future health status used by insurers when applying for Medigap plans outside of guaranteed issue periods.

CLOSING NOTE FROM MATT

Thanks for sticking with me.

If you've made it this far, you've done something most people never do, you've taken the time to actually learn how Medicare works behind the scenes. You didn't just pick a plan from a postcard or a TV ad. You looked under the hood. That puts you ahead of the game.

When I left the corporate Medicare world, I made a promise: to give people the truth about how this stuff really works. Not the version you get from a commercial, or a sales pitch, or a one-size-fits-all call center script. The version I saw from the inside.

That's why I wrote this book. And it's why I created the *Prepare for Medicare Insider Method*™ to help people avoid mistakes, save money, and feel confident about their choices.

If this book helped you, there's more where it came from. I've got step-by-step online courses, consumer guides, newsletters, and live support available at <u>PrepareforMedicare.com</u>. Ok, last time! You can also schedule a no-obligation call with Niki or one of our trusted advisors at <u>BrickhouseAgency.com</u> if you're ready to talk through your options.

Either way, you don't have to figure this out alone.

Medicare may not be exciting, but it's one of the most important financial decisions you'll make in retirement. I'm glad you took it seriously. And I'm proud to be part of your journey.

Stay smart. Stay prepared. And don't be afraid to ask for help when you need it.

– Matt

WHO IS MATT FERET?

Matt Feret began his professional career in live television news reporting and anchoring in and around rural Virginia, Missouri, Kentucky, and Illinois before going back to graduate school. While in school, he got a customer service job at the local Blue Cross and Blue Shield plan to help pay for tuition. It was there that he discovered his passion for directly and personally helping people navigate the healthcare and retirement maze.

He's made professional stops at Elevance Health, Humana, HCSC, CVS Health/Aetna and Medical Mutual. The thoughts and opinions expressed in this publication are those of the author only and are not the thoughts and opinions of any current or former employer of the author. Nor is this publication made by, on behalf of, or endorsed or approved by any current or former employer of the author.

Matt really loves his wife and kids who tolerate living with him in Chicagoland. The family also includes a cat, Puck, who was apparently named after a Shakespeare character. His kids made him add Puck's name to this bio.

Matt loves public and private speaking-come connect with him on the interwebs!

Company Name:
MF Media, LLC

Email:
mf@mattferet.com

Websites:
https://PrepareforMedicare.com

https://PrepareforSocialSecurity.com

https://TheMattFeretShow.com

LinkedIn:
linkedin.com/in/mattferet

Facebook:
https://www.facebook.com/PrepareforMedicare

More Books by Matt Feret:
https://www.amazon.com/author/mattferet

www.ingramcontent.com/pod-product-compliance
Lightning Source LLC
Chambersburg PA
CBHW050511210326
41521CB00011B/2411